This book belongs to:

_____

Table of Contents

Chapter 1 - The Little Boy with Big Dreams — 5

Chapter 2 - The Boy at Barcelona — 13

Chapter 3 - Becoming Barcelona's Brightest Star — 21

Chapter 4 - Beyond the Field — 29

Chapter 5 - Messi, The Family Man — 37

Chapter 6 - Messi's Philanthropy — 45

Chapter 7 - Messi's Culinary Passion — 53

Chapter 8 - A Rosarian in Paris — 61

Bonus Chapter - The Crown Jewel — 69

The stories you are about to read are grounded in real life, reflecting the triumphs and trials of individuals who dared to dream. While these narratives are rooted in truth, we've taken care to respect privacy and avoid overt promotion by altering certain trademarked terms in illustrations. Dive in and let these tales inspire you, as they have been inspired by the world around us. Enjoy this journey, where truth is often more fascinating than fiction.

The Little Boy with Big Dreams

CHAPTER 1

Once upon a time, in the buzzing, soccer-crazed city of Rosario, Argentina, a tiny tot named Lionel Messi fell in love with soccer. He was barely taller than the patched-up ball he played with, but he had a dream bigger than anyone could imagine. His tiny feet danced around the ball, dust swirling up from the small, worn-out field that became his very own grand stadium.

Each thump of the ball against his foot echoed in his heart — a rhythm that pulsed with his love for the beautiful game. Despite the world around him bustling with life, when Messi was with his soccer ball, all he heard was the sound of his heartbeat echoing his dream, a dream to conquer the soccer world.

Despite his smaller stature, Messi's talent on the field was gigantic. He was a whizz on the field, his short legs running rings around his friends, the soccer ball practically attached to his feet as he weaved his way past pretend defenders. Even his taller and stronger friends could only watch in awe as little Messi made them look like towering giants frozen in time.

They began calling him "La Pulga" — "The Flea" because of his small size and quick, darting movements. Little did they know, their friend was destined for a future where he would leap over every obstacle that came his way, just like a flea.

At just six years old, Messi took the first giant step towards his dream — he joined his first club, Grandoli, where his father Jorge was a coach. The club was small and its resources were limited, but for Messi, it was the stage he needed.

Here, under the watchful eyes of his father and with the cheers of his proud mother echoing in his ears, Messi began transforming from a boy with a dream into a player with a mission. He learned about teamwork, tasted the sweetness of victory, and experienced the bitterness of defeat. His journey wasn't just about winning or losing; it was about falling in love with the beautiful game, again and again, every single day.

The Boy at Barcelona

CHAPTER 2

At only 13 years old, Lionel Messi had to make a big choice that would change his life. He had a chance to try out for Barcelona, one of the top soccer teams in the world. Leaving his home in Argentina was hard for Messi and his family, but the thought of playing for Barcelona was too exciting to pass up. Even though they had to move to a new country, and Messi had to learn a new language, he and his family made the brave choice to go.

It was tough, but Messi found comfort on the soccer field. It was there where he could let his incredible skills do all the talking.

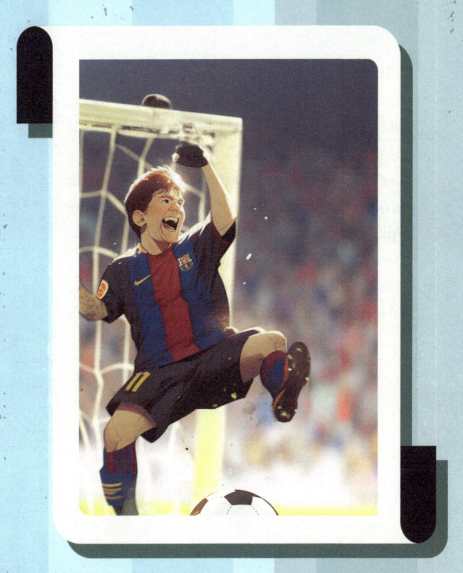

Barcelona has a famous youth academy called La Masia, known for training great soccer players. Messi got to learn their unique style of play called "tiki-taka". This style focuses on keeping the ball by passing it a lot and moving around constantly. Messi was a natural fit for "tiki-taka". His amazing skills blossomed and he began to stand out among his peers. Messi was becoming more than just a good soccer player; he was becoming an artist of the game.

Messi's first game for Barcelona's top team came when he was just 17, in a match against Espanyol. This was a moment that had been years in the making, the result of many hours of training and hard work. From the moment he stepped onto the field, Messi made a big impression. His quick thinking and sharp vision were beyond his years. Not long after, Messi scored his first goal - a clever chip shot over the goalkeeper.

This amazing moment showed everyone that Messi was a future soccer star. The young boy who had left his home in Argentina with dreams of playing professional soccer was now a sensation. Lionel Messi had shown the world what he could do.

Becoming Barcelona's Brightest Star

CHAPTER 3

In an amazing game against Getafe, Messi dodged past five players from the other team. He then scored a goal that made people all over the world say, "Wow!" This fantastic goal reminded many others of a famous goal that Diego Maradona, another player from Argentina, scored during the 1986 World Cup.

This led to Messi getting the nickname "Messidona". Messi, who is a very humble guy, was fast becoming the best player for Barcelona. He was dazzling everyone with his super soccer skills.

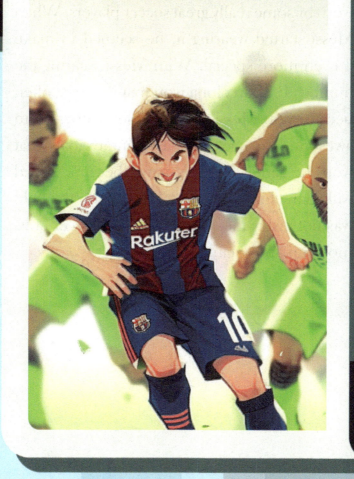

The number 10 jersey at Barcelona has been worn by some really great soccer players. When Messi started wearing it, he seemed to make it even more special. With Messi wearing the number 10, Barcelona won many games, often because of Messi's incredible skills. From awesome free-kicks to last-minute goals that won the games, Messi's name became linked with Barcelona's success. His play on the field was not just game-changing; it was soccer at its most fun and exciting.

In 2012, Messi did something many people thought was impossible — he broke the record for most goals scored in a single year. The old record was held by a player named Gerd Müller. Messi scored an amazing 91 goals, which left people all around the world amazed. This showed how great Messi was and pushed the limits of what people thought could be done in soccer. Messi's skills, hard work, and love for soccer made him not just the best player for Barcelona, but a true legend of the game.

Beyond the Field

CHAPTER 4

The exciting rivalry between Lionel Messi and Cristiano Ronaldo is a big part of modern soccer. They play the game differently, which makes their matches very interesting. Ronaldo uses his strength and speed, while Messi uses his skills and quick thinking. When they play against each other, it's like watching a superhero showdown. It's thrilling for soccer fans all over the world.

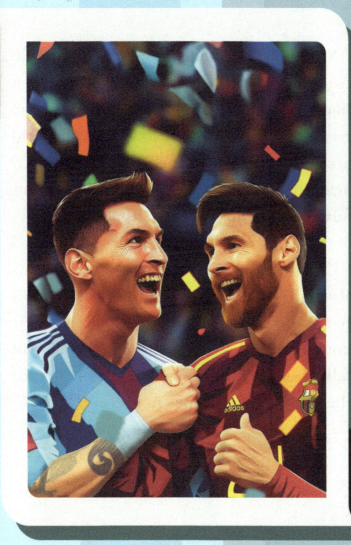

Messi and Ronaldo always try to outdo each other. This helps them play even better. Messi's awesome goals, his perfect passes, and his fantastic moves on the field are magical. Every time Barcelona played against Real Madrid, it was like a new adventure in this great rivalry.

Even though they're rivals, Messi respects Ronaldo a lot. He admires Ronaldo's hard work and dedication to soccer. Their competitiveness is so epic that people will talk about it for a long time during one of the most amazing times in soccer.

Away from the big stadiums and bright lights, Lionel Messi is a simple guy who loves his family very much. He met his wife Antonela Roccuzzo, when they were just little kids in Rosario, their hometown. Their friendship grew into love as they got older.

They got married in 2017, in a beautiful ceremony back in Rosario. This was the happy ending to their love story. Messi loves his family a lot. He's a caring husband and a fun dad to his three sons, Thiago, Mateo, and Ciro.

Messi, The Family Man

CHAPTER 5

Messi's Instagram is peppered with snippets of his family life, from beach trips to backyard soccer games with his sons. These simple moments, away from the public eye, are his cherished treasures, providing inspiration and strength. His relationship with his parents and siblings is just as close-knit.

Messi attributes his humble nature and the values he holds dear to their unwavering support. Despite his global fame and exceptional career, Messi has stayed true to his roots, always remembering the family who has stood by him in times of joy and adversity.

Messi's love for his family shines bright and clear. As a devoted father to his three sons, Thiago, Mateo, and Ciro, he fills his world with their joy and laughter. His Instagram is a vivid collection of the irreplaceable moments they share – frolicking trips to the beach, thrilling backyard soccer matches, and the quiet comfort of family dinners.

Messi, often standing in the global limelight, cherishes these instances away from the public's gaze. They act as his sanctuary, his tranquil retreat. They replenish his spirit, infuse him with unmatched strength, and provide a heartening reminder of what he strives for, a happy, loving family.

The bond that Messi shares with his parents and siblings holds a unique significance in his life. Their influence has shaped his humble disposition and instilled in him values that he treasures. Despite the international fame, the blinding spotlight, and the constant scrutiny that follows him, Messi stays true to his roots. His family serves as a grounding force, a safe harbor amidst the choppy seas of his professional life.

Their unwavering support through every hurdle and every triumph has been instrumental in his journey. Messi acknowledges this wholeheartedly, always remembering his origins and the people who have stood by him. From Rosario to Barcelona, and now Paris, Messi's bond with his family remains unbroken, testifying to their pivotal role in his life.

Messi's Philanthropy

CHAPTER 6

You may already know about Messi's extraordinary skills on the soccer field. But did you know that he's also a superhero off the field? Yes, that's right! In 2007, Messi started a special mission, the Leo Messi Foundation. Think of it as a superhero force that helps children who need it most.

The mission of this foundation is to ensure that children can go to school and have access to the health care they need. Messi, who grew up dreaming about playing soccer in a small town in Argentina, strongly believes that every child should have the chance to follow their dreams, just like he did.

The story of the Leo Messi Foundation's work is nothing short of amazing. The foundation has embarked on a series of projects that have brought joy and relief to many children. For instance, they've taken the initiative to rebuild schools in war-torn Syria, giving children a safe place to learn and play. Additionally, in Messi's homeland of Argentina, the foundation has helped children get crucial heart surgeries.

These kids, who were once struggling, now have hope and a chance at a healthier life, thanks to the foundation. But the Leo Messi Foundation doesn't work alone in its mission to help children. It teams up with other generous organizations, such as **UNICEF**, to make a bigger impact in the world and help even more children in need.

Messi's kindness doesn't stop with his foundation's work. It extends all the way back to his hometown, Rosario. If you remember, that's where he started playing soccer, at a club called Newell's Old Boys. Messi hasn't forgotten his roots or the place that helped shape him into the superstar he is today. To show his appreciation, he has helped Newell's Old Boys build a new gymnasium and a dormitory for their young players.

For Messi, helping his community, the place he once called home, is a source of immense pride. He's not just saying thank you, but he's also passing on the help and support he received. Messi's story shows us that true success is not only about personal achievements, but it's also about lifting others and making a positive difference in their lives. Isn't it wonderful how Messi is not just a soccer hero, but a real-life hero too?

Messi's Culinary Passion

CHAPTER 7

When he's not playing soccer, Lionel Messi has a special love for food and cooking. This shows in a restaurant he co-owns, called 'Bellavista del Jardín del Norte', which is in the middle of Barcelona. This friendly place reflects Messi's roots in Argentina, serving tasty meals that blend Argentinian and Mediterranean styles.

When you walk into the restaurant, you can see lots of soccer memorabilia, reminding you of Messi's amazing career. Each item tells a story of Messi's adventures in soccer. The delicious food and exciting atmosphere make you feel like you're stepping into Messi's world.

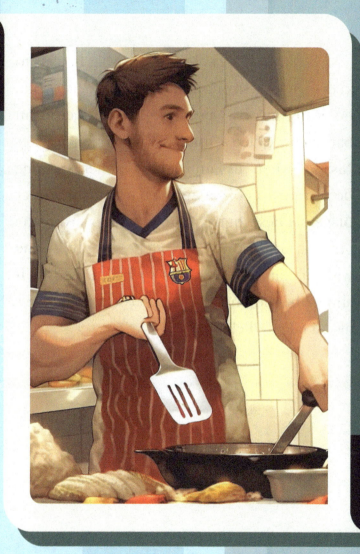

Messi has to be careful about what he eats to keep his body strong and ready for soccer. But, he really loves a special kind of Argentinian barbecue called "asado". He often makes "asado" when his family gets together, showing he's a great cook as well as a brilliant soccer player. These quiet moments away from the crowds and the soccer pitch, spending time with his family, are really special to Messi. It shows that he's not just good at soccer, but he's also a talented chef.

Even though Messi eats healthily most of the time, he loves sweet treats too. His favorite dessert is the 'Milhojas', a yummy Argentinian pastry. It's made of layers of creamy filling between thin, crispy pastry. Messi's love for this dessert shows how much he cherishes his Argentinian roots. Even when he's playing soccer in cities like Barcelona and Paris, Messi's heart is still in Argentina. His love for 'Milhojas' is a tasty reminder of his strong connection to his homeland.

A Rosarian in Paris

CHAPTER 8

In the summer of 2021, something very unexpected happened in Lionel Messi's life. Because of money problems, Barcelona, the soccer team Messi had been a part of since he was 13 years old, couldn't keep him. This news was really tough for Messi, his teammates, and the many fans of Barcelona all over the world. For lots of people, Messi wasn't just a player for Barcelona — he was like the heartbeat of the team.

When he left, it was like the end of a special time that had so many wins, amazing moments, and awesome soccer games that felt like magic. There were lots of tears and sad goodbyes because Messi had meant so much to Barcelona.

Even though leaving Barcelona was very hard, Messi was ready for a new adventure with Paris Saint-Germain (PSG), another really good soccer team with big dreams. It was strange to see Messi in a PSG jersey instead of the Barcelona one everyone was used to seeing him in. But no matter what jersey he wore, one thing never changed — Messi's deep love for soccer.

He tackled the challenge of getting used to a new team and a new city with the same toughness and never-give-up attitude that he showed as a young boy in his hometown, Rosario. This showed just how determined Messi is, and reminded everyone that the young boy who fell in love with soccer in a small town in Argentina was still the same.

In Paris, Messi got to play with Neymar again, an old friend from his time at Barcelona. The idea of watching these two incredible soccer players team up again was super exciting for soccer fans everywhere. They couldn't wait to see the fantastic moves, the perfect passes, and the amazing goals that Messi and Neymar would create together.

As Messi got used to his new life in Paris, he was still the same soccer-loving guy. With the spirit of the young boy from Rosario still strong in his heart, Messi was ready to start the next part of his awesome soccer journey.

The Crown Jewel: Argentina's World Cup Victory

BONUS CHAPTER

In the unforgettable year of 2022, the lively streets of Argentina echoed with joyful shouts and cheers. Flags of sky blue and white, the colors of the nation, swirled in the wind as a fantastic story unfolded. Argentina, guided by the amazing soccer star Lionel Messi, won the biggest prize in soccer, the FIFA World Cup.

It was a nail-biting game against France, held under the bright sun of Qatar. It was a test of skill, teamwork, and courage that had everyone watching biting their nails. In the end, Argentina won the day, scoring 4-2 in the super exciting penalty shootout.

For Messi, this victory meant more than just another win. It was a dream come true, a dream that he had held close since he was a young boy kicking a worn-out soccer ball. Winning the World Cup was the highlight of his career, which was already full of awesome achievements, like winning the prestigious Ballon d'Or.

The Ballon d'Or, which means 'Golden Ball' in French, is a yearly event that celebrates the best male soccer player in the world. It's like the 'Best Actor' award but for soccer players. Messi has won the reputable awards several times! Each win made him even more recognized as one of the best players in the world.

But this World Cup win was the cherry on top. It was the highest point of his soccer career, showing off his never-give-up attitude, awesome soccer skills, and deep love for his home country.

His journey, marked by determination, incredible talent, and a love for the game, teaches us that dreams really can come true. Whether it's the worn-out shoes of a young boy in Rosario or the gleaming golden trophy of the FIFA World Cup, Messi's story is proof that with passion, skill, and a never-give-up spirit, anyone can become a legend. Messi isn't just a soccer player, he's a role model, a leader, and above all, a true champion.

The End

We hope you enjoyed our book! If you could take a moment to leave a rating for us, it would greatly help us. Your feedback not only supports our work but also helps other readers. Thank you!

Made in the USA
Las Vegas, NV
02 February 2024

85207618R00046